ISBN 1-85576-009-6
Illustrations copyright © 1990 Gerald Hawksley
Text copyright © 1990 Treehouse Children's Books Ltd
Published by Treehouse Children's Books Ltd 1990
All rights reserved
Printed in Spain by Salingraf, S. A. L.

JO'S GARAGE

Words by Caroline Cary
Pictures by Gerald Hawksley

TREEHOUSE

This is Jo and Watcha, Jo's dog.
Jo is a mechanic.
Watcha likes to watch Jo working.

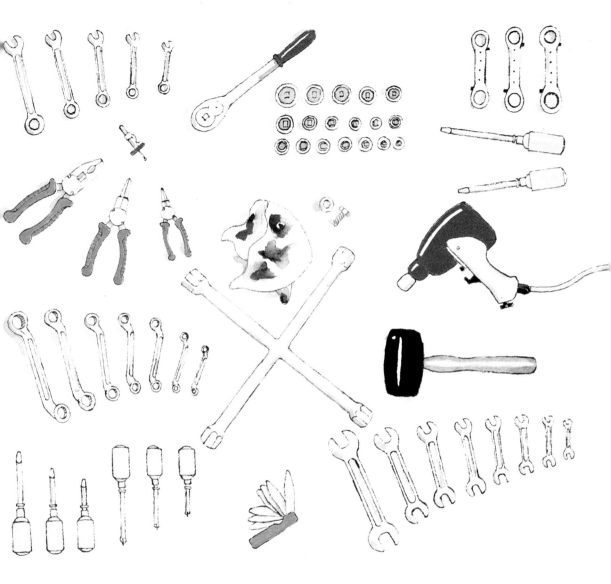

These are the tools Jo needs to mend the cars
in her garage.
What do they all do?

ramp

"This car needs a new exhaust pipe," says Jo.
VROOOM! Jo drives the car on to her ramp.
She pulls a lever.
MMMMMMMMMM . . . up goes the car.

air wrench

POPAPOPAPOPAPOP . . . Jo switches on the compressor. It powers her air wrench. ZIP . . . ZIP . . . the air wrench undoes all the nuts and bolts.

spanner

One bolt won't undo. Jo uses a spanner.
She pulls hard.
''Oof,'' says Jo. The nut turns. ''Done it,'' says Jo.
''Woof,'' barks Watcha, and wags his tail.

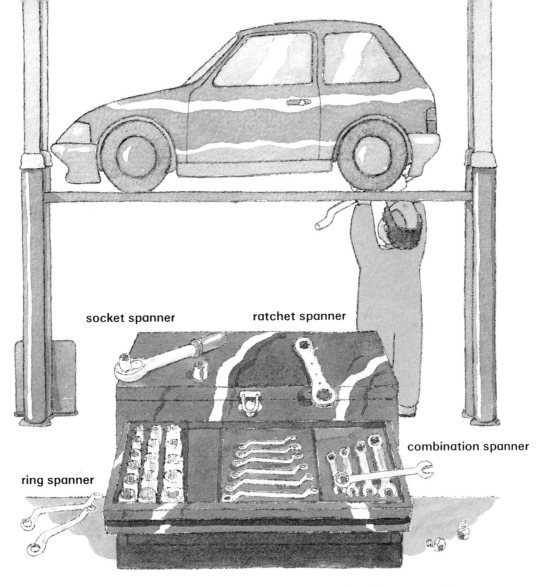

socket spanner

ratchet spanner

combination spanner

ring spanner

Jo keeps all kinds of spanners in her toolbox.
She has one for every size of bolt.
She fits the new exhaust pipe.
ZIP . . . ZIP . . . goes the air wrench.

tyre gauge

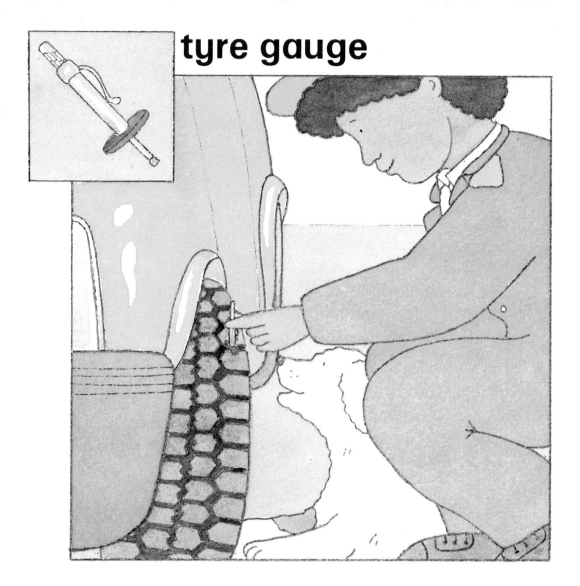

"I think this car has a worn out tyre," says Jo.
"Go and fetch my tyre gauge, Watcha."
Jo measures the depth of the tread with
the tyre gauge.

trolley jack

"This tyre needs changing," says Jo. She lifts the wheel off the ground with her trolley jack. ZIP . . . ZIP . . . she unscrews the nuts with her air gun, and takes off the wheel.

airline

Jo puts a new tyre on the wheel.
She blows it up with air from the airline.
SSSSSS . . . Watcha doesn't like the noise.
A gauge tells Jo when she has put in enough air.

wheelbrace

Jo puts the wheel back on the car.
She screws up the nuts with a wheelbrace
because the air wrench would screw
them up too tight.

engine analyser

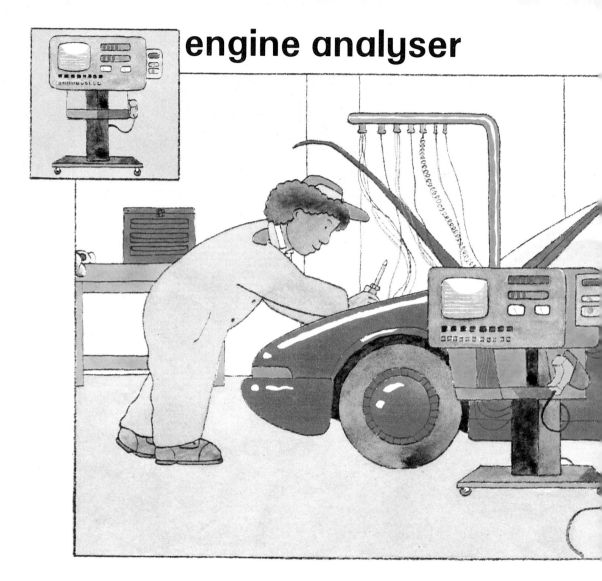

"Listen to the noise this engine makes," says Jo.
MMMPOPMMMPOPMMMPOP . . . goes the engine.
"My engine analyser will tell me what
the trouble is."

screwdriver

The engine analyser tells Jo that
a screw needs adjusting.
She turns the screw with a screwdriver.
MMMMMMMMMMMMMM . . . goes the engine.

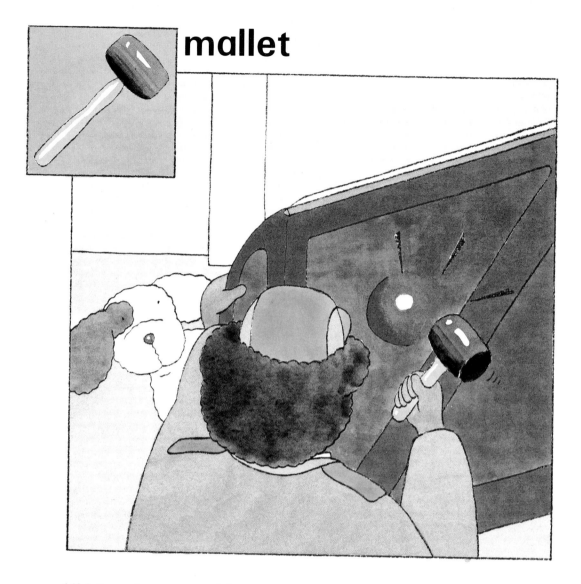

mallet

''What's next, Watcha?'' asks Jo.
''Ah yes, Mrs. Maloney's car has a nasty dent
and a scratch in the door.'' Jo knocks out the
dent with a mallet . . . TAP . . . TAP . . .

spray gun

Jo paints over the scratch with her spray gun.
SHHHHHHHH . . . goes the spray gun.
''Soon it will look like new,'' boasts Jo.
''I can fix anything.''

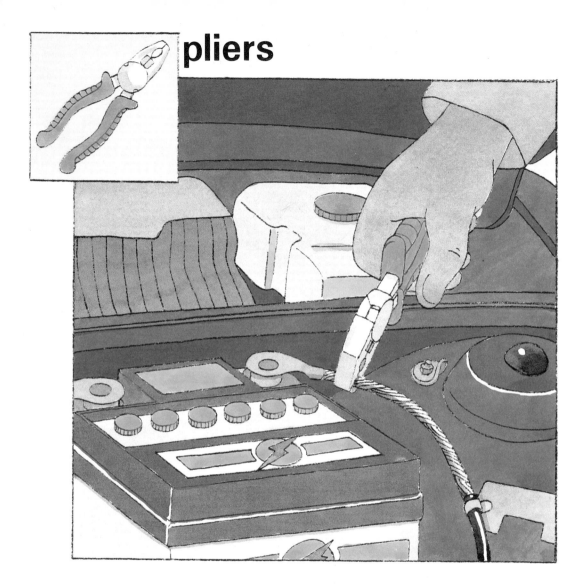

pliers

"This car won't work at all," says Jo.
Jo checks that the wires are connected.
She grips them with her pliers.
"Nothing wrong there," says Jo.

feeler gauge

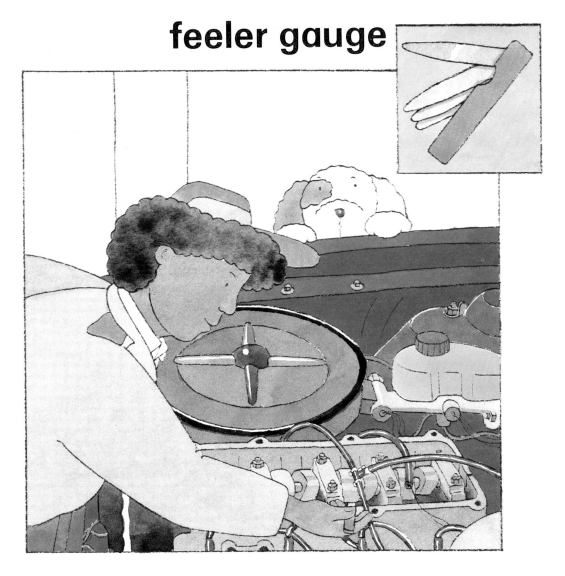

Jo checks the engine with a feeler gauge.
It measures the tiny gaps between the parts.
Jo sees that everything is in the right place.
''It should work,'' says Jo, scratching her head.

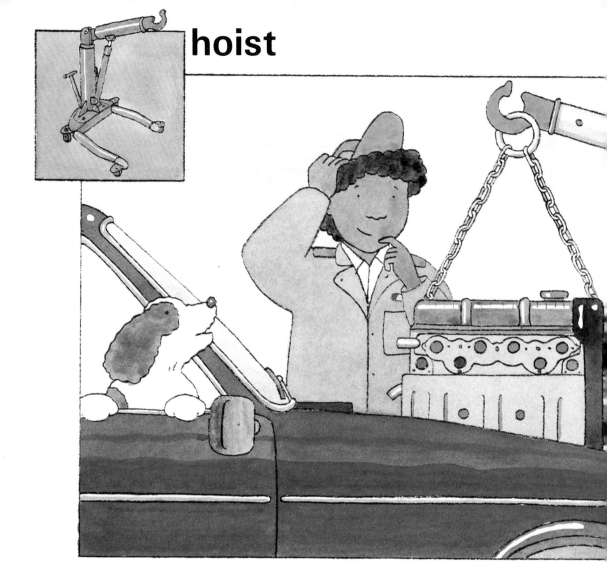

hoist

"Oh dear, I'll have to lift out the engine
with my hoist, and look inside," says Jo.
She unbolts the engine.
But she can't find anything wrong.

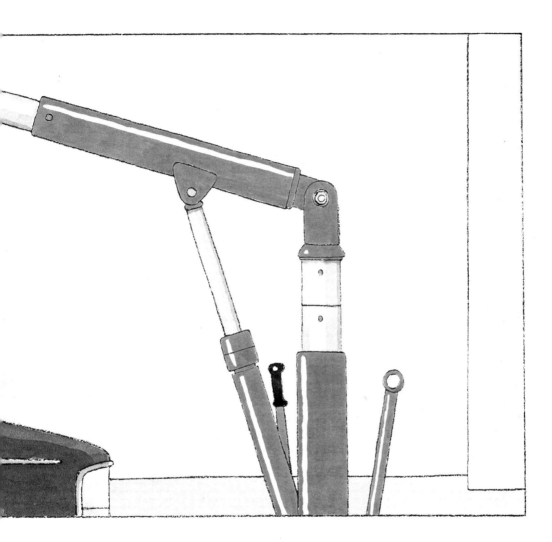

Jo puts the engine back in the car.
CHUG . . . CHUG . . .
It still won't start.
''What can the matter be?'' says Jo.

"Woof," says Watcha.
"What's that?" asks Jo. Watcha has a petrol can.
"Of course, it's run out of petrol," laughs Jo.
"Well done, Watcha. WE can fix anything."